Magnificent Love
The End Really The Beginning

Copyright © 2016 Jonathan Dekle

All rights reserved.

ISBN: 0-692-74583-1

ISBN-13: 978-0-692-74583-0

All rights reserved.

No part of this publication may be reproduced, distributed, or transmitted in any form or by any means, including, photocopying, recording, or any other form of electronic or mechanical methods, without the prior written permission of the publisher, except in the case of brief quotations embodied in critical reviews and certain other noncommercial uses. For other uses, seek permission requests by writing to the publisher, addressed "Attention: Permissions Coordinator," at the address below.

www.jonathandekle.com Via Contact Us

Live On

One Love God

Value Life

Everyday Counts

Over power Negativity

Never give up

#LoveOnForever
#LoveOn
#HeartVibes
#LoveVibes
#PositiveVibes

OTHER PUBLISHED WORKS BY **JONATHAN DEKLE** AVAILABLE VIA **AMAZON**

MAGNIFICENT LOVE: THE END REALLY THE BEGINNING

||

MAGNIFICENT LOVE: PERSONAL STRUGGLES

||

FOREVER LOVE YOU: LOVE ON

||

Others will be coming as time goes on:

SO GO ONLINE AND IN THE SEARCH ENGINE ON **AMAZON**, TYPE IN
Jonathan Dekle

Visit also my website @ jonathandekle.com

Thank you, may love carry us on.

Dedication

In this book you shall read about the realities to life.

Hear about the connections to actual life.

Will think about our most inner personal thoughts imaginable.
The thoughts we sometime never can answer.

This book is designed to enlighten all and be a guide to wisdom.

For wisdom is the key to freedom.

This book is made to reread over and over.

For each time you read,

New understanding comes with.

I am only a messenger.

A human being just as you.

Life is an adventure, a journey.

Journey on with me,

Will you?

To the unlock questions with answers.

CONTENTS

Acknowledgments	i
Examine Life?	1
Lessons	2
Self or Together?	3
Steps	4
Strange One	5
Who Are You?	6
Choose Your Fight	7
Jump	8
Beauty	9
Smoothness	10
Fighting Self	11
Daily Fight	12
Know Yourself	13
You Wonder	14
I See — Do You?	15
Reflection	16
Your Gift	17
Simple	18
Truly Unstoppable	19
Your Amazing	20
Think	21
We Together	22
Life	23
The Drive	24
I Share	25
That Moment	26

Small Things	27
Alive	28
To Feel	29
The Heavens	30
The Knock	31
Sun Rise Daily	32
Future Past	33
First Time	34
The Race	35
Review it All	36
Life's Meaning	37
Golden Rule	38
Branching Out	39
You Inspire	40
Actions	41
Echo's Reminders	42
Perfectionist	43
The Journey	44
Choose	46
Quality	47
Ask Yourself	48
Be Happy	49
Warning Signs	50
Life's Groove	51
Design	52
Your Value	53
It's Those Small Things	54
Misjudged	55
Finding Clarity	56

BOOK TITLE

Time	57
Perfect Timing	58
Help	59
To Understand	60
Clear	61
Outside	62
Enlightenment	63
Future Seen	64
Mindset	65
Old Home	66
To Love	67
True Success	68
Colors	69
Words Impact	70
Teamwork	71
Find Yourself	72
Vibes	73
Your Belief	74
Lemonade	75
Ghostly	76
Impulse	77
Fear	78
Value of Love	79
The Heart	80
Rock bottom	81
Yearly Reflection	82
Viewpoints	83
Guaranteed	84
Push	85
Love Rules	86

Genuine Love	87
Forever Love	88
Over Obsessively Done	89
Church	90
The Fallen Risen	91
Sharing	92
Beauty in Life	93
New Beginnings	94
You Choose Life's View	95
Love is in Us	96
God is Love	97

Examine Life?

The more you see something,
The more clarity you also see too.
For you slowly get to see more in depth to it.
Sometimes it may take a hundred looks,
But slowly you begin to see new wonders and beauty behind it.
For you are seeing just truly how amazing each thing has such complexity;
Such individual creativity,
That you start to see its wholeness and its uniqueness,
Thus its true meaning.
—J. Micheal Dekle

Lessons

I can master something and fail at another thing.
I can be a dragon.
I can be a wimp.
I can jump and see stars;
I can get down and see nothing.
I can have hope;
I can have no clue what's going to happen next though.
I jump and hope.
I can do anything always having this courage behind me.
Knowing,
As long as I remember I'm only human,
I can always try better next time.
I will cry and shed a tear if it means I learned.
I'll forgive and forget and move on if I know we can all embrace something even better yet.
The key is: —
If we know there always is another day and another chance to show we can do something greater,
We then can truly become heroes.
—J. Micheal Dekle

Self or Together?

We walk into life proud.
We act like we are bosses,
But deep down understand,
We are helpless.
We talk like we can do anything,
But know we can only try to.
We try to put two and two together and create friendships into relationships,
Into brotherhood and sisterhood,
Thus true family.
We grow, we separate.
But we never forget deep down who was real and who was just a faze.
We day dream of those days.
Wish we could just go back for one minute and moment to fix things.
Change things.
We wish we could climb over and back into time to cherish the moments just a little bit more.
We look ahead and know we can do better,
We can become better, and we can live each day and see the special moments and appreciate them more for they are precious.
—J. Micheal Dekle

Steps

We take one step.
Then we take two steps,
Then three,
Four,
Five,
Until—
Soon we don't even know how many we took.
It's the same way when we learn.
We slowly take those steps until we don't even think about it;
We just do it.
So take as many steps in life as possible because after the challenge of learning is done.
You just advanced your possibilities in every aspect of life by becoming someone and something greater;
So thus you become more knowledgeable and useful and understanding for your next challenge.
—J. Micheal Dekle

Strange One

As a strange one I stand aside.
As one who see things differently,
I am cast out and turned into something and someone many do not like.
For they know I will always have something to say that's unpredictable,
That's different;
That isn't always likable.
Fight on I must do with people and demons,
Always carrying a burden of pain and sorrow;
For what I see saddens me and weighs me down,
For I know tomorrow won't be any better,
But worst,
For we truly live in a living nightmare.
But what lifts me up is I know no matter what load I must carry now,
I will only become stronger and wiser,
For I know my reward will be eternal life because at all given moments I have only one true friend,
And one person who will always show love,
and that is Jesus.
—J. Micheal Dekle

Who Are You?

As a ghost you get to view without being known.
As a wave you get to touch anything and everything in your zone.
As a mountain you get to pick out the weak and see who's the strong motivated one.
As a clone you get to only follow and say nothing but yes ma'am, yes sir.
So.........
Who are you?
—J. Micheal Dekle

Choose Your Fight

Sometimes I wonder if I did the right thing,
If I made the right move.
In life you can't wait around forever;
If something isn't functional you fix it,
and do so fast.
If it can't be fixed,
You move on to things that can be fixed.
Things with sentimental attachments though,
In my belief should never be forgotten,
But sometimes they have to be set free so the new can come in.
—J. Micheal Dekle

Jump

As we jump into life;
We must try and do so with passion:
With care,
With respect,
With thought,
And with God by our side.
So when we do something we know we won't just do it.
We will conquer it and make it to the upmost
we can.
For we do so to please our Maker,
Thus so,
Pleasing everyone.
—J. Micheal Dekle

Beauty

Some may ask what determines beauty.
Others think they know beauty;
But to truly measure such a gifted gift as beauty,
You have to appreciate it.
Have to love it.
Have to respect it.
Admire and overview all aspects.
Thus your own dice of beauty is made,
Is determined.
—J. Micheal Dekle

Smoothness

As I sit and look at the Chinese make my food.
I look upon how cheerful and happy they are.
I notice how team organized they work.
Notice they must be family.
For they truly inter act as one.
Even though in the mist of their busy business,
They handle it like champions.
—J. Micheal Dekle

Fighting Self

Some days I'll be like just bla—
Others —
Just ba —
Na—
Why should I care?
Why should I continue trying?
Frustration develops into angry,
Into confusion of mix wired feelings,
To uncertainty of why this or they do that.
But my higher self steps in and knows no matter how immature or mistreated I was,
Or how mislead my thoughts were,
That I must stand as the higher person always;
So to lead the way,
To show the mature,
Caring,
Loving way.
So at least someone is being the light bearer;
So the good can stay shining to brighten up this world,
But more overly,
So others can see a difference of behavior,
So they too,
Can learn to develop into someone greater.
—J. Micheal Dekle

Daily Fight

Each day I battle to fight against myself.
Some days I lose and choose to hammer myself down,
So I learn my mistakes by having to deal with its pain as a reminder;
But I always remember them so I do not make them again as easily.
For to stand as a true being,
You have to recognize your mistakes
And by so doing,
You're only becoming more real and a more knowledgeable person of
true character;
That truly was built into a statue of stone that was hand
carved and chipped,
So when tested, you will not move,
But stand firm in all aspects because you been there,
Done that,
And know true wisdom;
For you learned from your past mistakes and took account of failure as a
blessing rather than a disappointment.
—J. Micheal Dekle

Know Yourself

When being put down by anyone—
Always remember,
They either are jealous,
Or—
Simply want to make everyone feel just as bad as they do about themselves.
—J. Micheal Dekle

You Wonder

I truly am the biggest monster I know.
Who controls who?
I some days really wonder....
But I have faith God will always hold me together,
No matter what!
So even if some days I wonder,
Even lose myself—
I still know God watch's over all,
and protects.
So when you wonder;
Let God show you the reflection of your wonder,
And turn that into power of transformation—
Or acceptance if need be.
—J. Micheal Dekle

I See — Do You?

What others see from you and what you see in yourself will always be different.
Usually others are only seeing twenty-five to thirty-five percent of someone.
For we all are growing,
Thus we all have to slowly release our inner self out into real actual life.
Some I believe who are seen as weird or 'different' are the ones who release more of themselves out because they are not afraid to be themselves
So they live fully on all that they can and want to be,
And that energy is shown.
—J. Micheal Dekle

Reflection

Sometimes I close my eyes just to go back to way back when all I saw was beauty at every turn.
I open them and feel refreshed knowing there still lie days like that ahead.
Time goes by and the sky stays the same till night falls and blackness;
The stars show new sights rotating- fixing the mess by beauty from above.
Love sounds and I turn and look to see what comes next.
I hope I see beauty.
See life with wonder and honor.
I plunder the hills and fields just so I can find that moment,
That heavenly palace of peace where I can release my pain,
My sorrows,
My headache of problems;
So I can go on unashamed and rock solid head high waving my crown of joy,
Happiness,
And honor because I found hope.
Found God still waving his flag so to brag and nag a tad that He still has all His nature named tagged.
That true love and life are still awaiting for anyone who chooses to grab hold of it—
That they too can have the gift of salvation waved and covered over themselves,
So they too can stand unashamed.
—J. Micheal Dekle

Your Gift

To write and express emotion into words is a gift,
For you're trapping life into words that will affect everyone
differently for timeless times to come.
Your actions somewhat do the same.
They effect everyone rather they want them to or not.
Leaving an impression and imprint on them for life.
Leaving your words and actions,
More precious than silver and gold.
—J. Micheal Dekle

Simple

Once you break things down it becomes simple.
Same with making anything,
Start off simple and slowly add and add 'till it's a master piece.
Same with doing a task,
Start it and don't think about its negative sides only its positive ones
'till completion.
—J. Micheal Dekle

Truly Unstoppable

That feeling of being unstoppable!
To gain such you first must believe in yourself,
Yet at the same time not get
too carried away and prideful,
But the opposite.
Cling to practice and discipline and learn how to push the
boundaries, but within reason;
Thus you begin to conquer the ideal of fearlessness and its
terminology;
Thus you truly start to become unstoppable.
When you add a huge mixture of God into the picture,
You truly are unstoppable to the utmost meaning of unstoppable.
—J. Micheal Dekle

You're Amazing

All of us have our uniqueness quelling amazing-ness,
Giving us that individual character that only people who know you can appreciate.
Hiding in a corner being a loner gets you absolutely nowhere but more incomplete and less self aware of your possibilities,
Entering into society tests you,
For then your always being enlightened by others,
Thus giving you more perspective on life itself,
Thus more overly allowing you to grow as a person either positively or negatively.
—J. Micheal Dekle

Think

Thinking is free.
Why not truly embrace its gift.
Why let others do your thinking for you?
We were made to be highly advance beings;
Designed for creative, compassionate loving,
To be sensible, inter-acting, selfless wanting beings,
To have care given thoughts,
To be released from our minds,
To only help us grow closer to each
other,
So we can understand each other better.
But more overly,
So love can be expressed,
And become real.
—J. Micheal Dekle

We Together

We live,
We die.
We improve,
Or we bring down.
We hide ourselves,
Or share our awesomeness with others.
We create a story each and every day,
Telling all who we are.
We stand united or divided.
We remember or forget.
We embrace or push away.
We are Americans.
We are people,
A people who accept all and any in the name of freedom—
So salute to all those who stand for freedom!
May we be united in one common goal.
In God We Trust—
Will We Stand Together?
—J. Micheal Dekle

Life

Life can be scary.
It can be blurry.
It can also be hurried on.
When hurricanes come and knock you down,
You can only stand back up and fight through them as the hero.
When we are tested,
We find who we truly are.
When we fall,
Many point and try to tear us apart,
And a part of you wants to fall even more.
But another part wants to throw your all into it,
To prove to all and any,
That they were wrong.
Vision pure success,
And it shall be yours.
Follow after righteousness,
And the flood gates of awesomeness will be yours.
Believe in what you do,
And whatever you do,
Eventually will become mastered.
Stand tall.
Be honored;
You have the chance to still choose who you want to be,
And thus become.
Never let go of love,
But store it away inside your heart;
So as life gets harder and harder you won't become harder and harder;
But softer and softer,
And more of a true, caring,
Compassionate person,
Because understanding and wisdom will become your best friend.
—J. Micheal Dekle

The Drive

We live to strive.
We strive to drive life.
Most drive the speed limit because they are afraid of the danger of
breaking loose from the normal.
Some push the boundaries,
Pushing on the craziness of creativity;
Combining and complicating common things,
To make them uncommon yet magical,
And different;
But all along,
Driving life,
Striving onward to make things better,
For they are not afraid of speeding,
But afraid of failing.
Who are you?
The follower of what has already been done and made,
Or the inventor and entrepreneur,
Pushing things on to the future?
—J. Micheal Dekle

I Share

I share because I care.
I see life is unfair so I move on to push for justice.
I know many are afraid,
So I stand as a warrior holding out all that is precious.
I press on knocking down walls people have trapped their selfish selves into recklessly,
Handing out knowledge.
I dodge the dodge balls thrown,
For I know who truly holds the golden crown at the end.
I don't pretend to be a friend to any,
For I am one to all.
If you call,
I shall come.
If you fall,
I shall help you up.
For we are family.
We are on the same team.
We face the same enemy.
Yes, we are mini by ourselves.
But with many of us together,
We can become overwhelmingly strong.
Holding on to love,
For love is what holds everything together.
—J. Micheal Dekle

That Moment

Everyone has that favorite moment of their day;
That special time they've been thinking about since they woke up,
That longing to just forget about everything holding them down-
that safe zone of comfort.
That my friends,
Is your bed.
That place you call your safety,
Your home.
For nothing beats a long day and being able to just lay back and
finally rest,
And for a brief moment not worry about a single thing.
Besides knowing you tired your best that very day to do what you
could to make it overwhelmingly beautiful and meaningful.
—J. Micheal Dekle

Small Things

Appreciate the small things.
Without them life would get tiring,
Boring,
And very depressing quickly.
The small things add up to be big;
The biggest things imaginable.
Add small gestures to life,
So life is fulfilling.
—J. Micheal Dekle

Aliveness

Not many things allow me to feel alive.
So those few things that let me feel alive,
I dive into with such energy it's crazy!
Always keeping in mind rather or not if it's in my best interests.
So life can be safe,
But plentifully fun and enjoyable.
—J. Micheal Dekle

To Feel

Nobody likes to feel unwanted,
To feel unappreciated,
To feel as though they aren't important, and not seen.
Everyone wants to be heard,
Wants to have a reason and purpose,
To be admired, respected and cared about.
Some days you may feel like nobody is there for you,
But I promise you,
Love is always there,
God is.
Yes, physical or seen affection is different.
But spiritual affection is so much stronger and powerful then anything imaginable.
That if we reach for it,
Our lives can be transformed into something stunningly beautiful.
—J. Micheal Dekle

The Heavens

In these last days
The only true peace I find is nature.
Nature still pressing on,
Looking up into the sky-
Seeing its stars flickering light upon us,
Letting us know there're others worlds beyond here,
That evil hasn't corrupted.
For we haven't even begun to know what real life is,
For we are trapped in a sin den prison, penned to this world until God comes,
Unless we seek the gift God has given us of eternal life where true peace always dwells.
We won't ever know of true long happiness.
—J. Micheal Dekle

The Knock

Faded, gone:
Some days I feel.
But coasting on I must go,
As a musket bullet fired.
Inspired,
Idling waiting for fire to overtake the mistakes I made.
Sword blade glazing,
Blazing,
Hazing down any overtakes of all wrongly done acts I committed.
Slowly fading,
Fazing each page,
And facing the sound of the music I created;
Surfacing as a new being,
Being only now brighter than ever.
Climbing out of my hell walls,
To climb up to my Heavenly Father's walls;
To call out down below to any fellow who is centered corned to the beast of the worldly sworn cursed horn.
Asking to all and any,
Do you want a new true re-beginning of being fully?
reborn?
Or does fading away to death row suit you happily,
To never again awaken?
Because you weren't shaken enough to find your senses to repent and understand it truly is the end of the world.
God is calling.
He is knocking.
Will you hear His call?
—J. Micheal Dekle

Sun Raise Daily

Sun rise to sun set we live.
We walk in the steps we created our life's to be.
Yes, we shaped them by each and every action leading to our final outcomes being how they are.
Yes, I tell the Lord to lead me on,
So I don't end up creating a fallen life.
But sometimes we invite the demon's hellish storms and selfish wants into our life.
Thus creating small hardships and miserable outcomes,
And question why things are the way they are,
Forgetting God's plan.
Yet even through such,
God can point out lessons to learn if we allow.
So once all is said and done,
You really didn't waste any time or pain if you then apply those lessons learned into effect and grow and become wiser from them and share with others how to dodge them.
Some ask: How are they so wise,
So knowledgeable?
It's simple: many have gone through hellish outcomes to live and tell the tale,
And now only try to warn you so you don't have to live through hell also.
Sun rise to sunset we live.
I choose to live happily.
How about you?
—J. Micheal Dekle

Future Past

Some wonder what I think about on a daily.
Usually I think of the future rather the past,
For my past usually saddens me deeply.
The future is what you make it to be.
The past isn't changeable.
Accept the past for what it is, a lesson book.
And make the future as beautiful as possible.
So one day you can think upon the past again and be filled with pleasant memories.
—J. Micheal Dekle

First Time

Nothing can ever compare to the first time something incredible was done.
When something is experienced the first time ever for someone,
The mind isn't knowing what to expect,
So the unknown is there,
That adventure and feeling of aliveness is.
And most importantly,
You yourself are fully there trying to take it all in.
You can because you're so drawn into it,
That for a brief moment,
You feel free,
And time isn't apparent;
Because time doesn't matter then.
In my eyes,
That's something truly remember-able and cherish-able for that's what life is all about,
Having breathtaking moments.
—J. Micheal Dekle

The Race

Fast pace moving;
Going—
Growing.
Slow pace seeing,
Feeling — Fleeing—
Pleading—
Crashing — Asking—
Uncovering—
Discovering the mathematical equations to all.
Repeating— bleeding—
Working —
Accomplishing until completed,
Finished.
For the sought after has clarity in the end.
For the life of the race was reached for,
Was fought for.
So the race truly was a battle to survive hardship,
Pain, suffering, tiredness, abandoned-ness,
And evil.
Remember to always keep our heads looking forward to our Maker,
So none of life's troubles can ever be too overwhelming,
But welcoming,
Because heaven is our true home.
So journey on we must,
To shine light on those who need it most!
To let love set us free!
—J. Micheal Dekle

Review it All

Factoring in all view points matter.
So does each detail.
For then the simple things can have such greater meaning and
beauty behind them,
For they are appreciated then more.
Seen as something precious and valuable.
Giving you perspective towards life in a larger way.
—J. Micheal Dekle

Life's Meaning

Life's not about being liked.
It's not about being the most popular or most powerful being, or richest.
It's simply about finding and creating who you will be and then standing by that person you choose to be.
Looking at yourself loving who you became and who you still will grow to become.
That's the meaning of life.
Remembering who controls all.
That we live in a fallen world.
So good and evil comes into play,
Either way we look at it,
We must never forget the meaning of life,
Which is accepting salvation.
For good and evil truly live in this world.
—J. Micheal Dekle

Golden Rule

Do unto others as you would like have done unto your deepest self
&
Treat others as you would like yourself to be treated,
It's the only true way to respect one another and yourself and live a happy life that's fulfilling and meaningful.
God created the Golden Rule to help guide us in love.
For nobody deep down wants to hurt themselves,
We all just want acceptance and love.
Be the love, the respect and role model.
—J. Micheal Dekle

Branching Out

The more you branch out,
The deeper your roots must be.
Roots in respect,
In love,
In God,
In just general life,
But especially in what branches you branch out as.
As in the more grounded as an individual you must be in whatever field of study you choose.
We all should study ourselves and know how to mentally, spiritually and physically control and best provide for ourselves just to stay healthy, it only makes sense.
For if you are not,
You will fall just as fast as you have raised by loosing your balance in life.
—J. Micheal Dekle

You Inspire

Having the ability to see perspective and stepping into someone
else's shoes surely isn't everybody's cup of tea.
But those lucky few who can,
Have the honor and power to channel into someone's heart to
touch them positively or negativity.
With great power,
Comes great responsibility.
I know for myself,
Some days I fail and falsely use my capabilities wrongly,
For any I may have put down,
I am sorry.
For those I have helped,
Keep on thriving and striving onward upward to a higher standard.
We never can be perfect.
We can only try to be.
Which what is what counts,
Trying to be.
Moving forward in the best way we know how to.
—J. Micheal Dekle

Actions

If someone can't see the whole you to you because they take things for grant,
It truly is a sad thing.
For they then are showing they are shallow and low and more over showing their true colors deep down which is selfishness.
We all want to be known and be seen as someone honorable and lovable.
But sometimes it's simply an illusion and the monster within shows more than the honorable and loving side;
Actions show and tell who you are.
Not words.
Words are meaningless unless actions also back them up.
—J. Micheal Dekle

Echo's Reminders

Echoes sound reminders—
Hellos sound emotional take ons to the echoes sounded—
What do I mean?
Past times bring in rushes of memories that nothing can compare to.
Present moments settle into a good day or to a bad day or to a remember-able day.
But either way echoes sound loudly.
As in music, pictures, smells, people, places etc.
It all can trigger past moments or create new trigging moments for the future.
And the hellos sound is you engaging into the past echoes and allowing the thoughts and memories lift your day up or to allow you to add on to a special memory.
Your ammunition is always loaded up so nobody can bring you down for you have your memories as company.
—J. Micheal Dekle

Perfectionist

I am selective,
And very picky.
It's because I am sensitive,
And have a taste that is very broad,
But also because I try to be a perfectionist.
When I buy something or see and do something,
I love to see that idea of perfectionist put into place,
Because then I can see passion,
Care and love was practiced and their number one principle in creating it was to perfect; was to please.
It's just how God is:
He doesn't only half do something,
He does it to its fullest maximum level.
He is selective with variety and max done creation that has its beauty in all forms,
But He perfects, and masters it,
Thus He is the truest perfectionist their ever will be.
How awesome is our God?
—J. Micheal Dekle

The Journey

I see and hear of people graduating,
Knowing that I should be among
those.
Many don't know or understand my past leading to my decisions to do
what I have done.
But I justify all I have done by knowing I got an education that no
school could ever offer,
And that is knowing real world functionality by being involved in it since
a very early age,
Developing workmanship,
Craftsmanship, discipline,
Team player associating, endurance,
Patience,
And understanding prosperity,
And probability and seeing reality as it really is
and my conclusion is this:
Life is short.
Money comes and goes.
Time flies by quicker then quick.
Balancing and grabbing onto education matters,
If you take it to heart.
Finding a passion and taking hold of it brings purpose.
Being calm and understanding people and things only makes you a
higher person.
Loving all outcomes and learning lessons from them only makes you
stronger.
God involved in your life gives you true peace.
Being a people's person gets you places.
Hobbies fills out boredom spells.
Saying something from the heart counts.
Saying please and thank you leaves a good impression.
Moving on forward instead of living in the past adds upon your life
rather than
living in the past staying in one spot holding you down.
Sharing knowledge never hurts.

You could die today,
So make each day as your last.
Meaning — doing what you said you would,
Holding onto moral grounds,
Shining off love and holding nothing,
But releasing everything,
Doing it to the best you can.
That the people that you know in your life are precious,
So don't take them half heartily, but fully.
Judge none, for each one of us are different and have our own battles
raging on within us.
Think before speaking.
Read before believing.
Always be polite.
Always love.
Always remember the positive moments.
Always stay true to yourself.
Finally: continue moving on forward to better all by living the Golden
Rule and following the Ten Commandments;
And I promise happiness will be
your end result.
—J. Micheal Dekle

Choose

I choose to smile and be thankful in all outcomes,
For I deserve to be happy,
For I am so blessed.
I just wish I could take any persons pain or burden away and share them Gods love to help fulfill them.
Imbuing some of my happiness with others,
For we all deserve to feel happy no matter the situation.
God.
Respect.
Goodness.
Reverence.
Revival.
Renewal.
Greatness.
Gratitude.
Grace.
Mercy.
Forgiveness.
Compassion.
Passion.
Faithfullness.
All quell into having everlasting happiness.
—J. Micheal Dekle

Quality

Some say if it gets the job done then it's okay.
Some say if you get the job done then it's also okay.
But I say quality is far better than anything else,
For then care is put into it.
Usually all the time it's worth the extra money to buy the better made thing.
And usually everyone is well pleased when someone does a good job,
For the end results shows someone cared what they were doing.
—J. Micheal Dekle

Ask Yourself

It's funny,
People know you when they know you can do something for them,
But forget you other times.
It's sad,
People think only upon themselves to gain supposedly a higher achievement in their own life;
But rarely think upon others to see if they can do so for them.
It's scary how low we have become;
But think we haven't,
When in reality we have become our own little monsters.
It's shameful how foolishly stupid we have become to simply accept anything and everything in society as though there isn't such a thing as good versus evil battling on around and between us.
It's heartbreaking how satanic we have become,
But still claiming God as who we follow;
When reality wise we have created our own form of God and worship.
If we stay on this pathway we find to be acceptable,
We surely will invite death itself into our doorways.
So ask yourself:
Does it pay to be lazy, and foolish, and ignore your Creator's commandments?
—J. Micheal Dekle

Be Happy

Life is what you make it.
You either look at its downfalls and downsides or you cling on to its
up sight forward-gestures and find contentment in all things.
For to just be alive is worthy of being happy:)
Always.
Be.
Happy.
—J. Micheal Dekle

Warning Signs

Looking, looking, upward, upward I look!
Awaiting, awaiting for the sky to shake!
I can't wait no longer for God to come!
All I see and feel is torment and disgust.
Evil truly is uprising on the daily.
We are living at the very end of time and God says nature shall show its signs.
God will warn people many last times by strange weather and unexplainable happenings.
They shall become more and more often as child labor is for a mother.
Stages surely have been rung!
Open your Bible and just please,
I beg of you give God a try; and I promise
you He will become real to you if you become real with Him.
That's a promise.
That His love.
His Word.
—J. Micheal Dekle

Life's Groove

Life is made to find your groove,
To create a pathway that stands out,
That slowly gets longer and wider,
So others can step in and be apart of it.
Each person will have their own pathway,
But there is only one pathway to Heaven,
And that is going through Jesus Christ to save us.
No person or any other being can save you except Jesus.
He is the only One who has the power to go to God and pardon our sins for us.
It's beautiful once you think about it.
God wants you to be fully you, and live in your groove,
Yet at the same time says He will walk with you through this rough life to the finish line if you let Him.
—J. Micheal Dekle

Design

Some of us are designed to share off our happiness,
And yet sometimes we can't,
For in that moment we aren't seeking after happiness,
Rather something else,
So we can't sponge any of it in,
Because it's foreign for the moment.
If we think of others before ourselves,
We usually are actually happier.
Because it's us following the Golden Rule.
So love is being shared and spread rather kept purely to ourselves.
—J. Micheal Dekle

Your Value

As long as you know who you are,
What you stand for,
What you're compassionate about,
And seeking out positively life;
Nothing can ever shake you,
For their opinion is simply an opinion.
Remember what's valuable;
Meaningful:
Not the uselessness that is meaningless.
What you focus on you will surely slowly become.
—J. Micheal Dekle

It's Those Small Things

It's the people and memories in life—
That are our truest riches that last forever.
That hold the highest value.
And is what holds us together.
It's those small things that add up to those huge things we couldn't
live without.
—J. Micheal Dekle

Misjudged

The Fallen,
But loved misjudged.
When they say God can only judge me now:
They are the people who's been so hurt,
So damaged,
And so mistreated by 'God fearing' people who are a disgraces to God—
That they block out everything people say,
For it by then means nothing,
For they literary don't care anymore.
Don't judge one another,
For by doing,
You're having God judge you doubled.
We are made to help build,
Not destroy.
Only love.
—J. Micheal Dekle

Finding Clarity

The feeling of finding clarity in the next steps you want to take.
The clarity gives you a power that's almost unstoppable,
For within the clarity comes confidence,
And within the confidences comes certainty in its reality.
—J. Micheal Dekle

Time

Past — Present — Future
Sometimes in life you have to put away the present you,
And hold onto the future you,
That you know there,
But just hasn't fully reached its prime to be the present you.
For sometimes the present you holds onto to much of the past you,
That it blinds you to the future you.
Life is all about balance, so balance how much time you invest your focus on.
—J. Micheal Dekle

Perfect Timing

It's absolutely incredible how life works out.
Leaving you knowing God is in control.
I have noticed,
It's in those moments were things seem to be falling completely apart,
Is when they start to make sense,
And the flight to a better place happens.
Sometimes when we hit those rock bottom moments and we feel like God Himself is even against us,
It is for us to grow stronger in faith.
And in the long run our trust in God grows, but also our reassurance in knowing God controls all does too.
—J. Micheal Dekle

Help

In order for you to receive help,
You must first be willing to receive it.
At the end of the day,
Nobody can help you but yourself.
We all will need help time to time,
And nothing is wrong with that.
Don't let your pride keep you away from reaching out for help.
Often times so many are willing to help us if we just say we need it.
—J. Micheal Dekle

To Understand

To understand anything or anyone you must be willing to try to step into their shoes,
Their pathway,
And their life to fully get a taste of it,
But also try to connect as much as your past experience emotions to it,
For its recognizable to you,
So you can relate to theirs almost magically.
—J. Micheal Dekle

Clear

Understand

Misunderstanding;
Miscommunication kills.
Open communication revives,
Grows each other closer together.
Helping to keep each other on the same page.
Be opened minded in conversations so no judgment is felt.
—J. Micheal Dekle

Outside

Going outside just for 15 minutes a day will improve all aspects of
your day and life.
Fresh air is life to our beings.
Why breathe in static air,
When it can be purely fresh.
Get outside,
It's ridiculously contagious.
—J. Micheal Dekle

Enlightenment

Enlightenment is the key to freedom.
The wise seek it out.
The fools cast it away.
The naive know no better.
Enlighten yourself, and be set free.
—J. Micheal Dekle

Future Seen

The happiest moments are looking and seeing pure progress
happening in the present,
Thus you know future,
Seeing real beauty from those moments of reflection of the past.
We can never fully know the future, but we can blue print it to a
degree, so to set a course to follow after.
Heaven is my home, so one part of life for me is to walk in Gods
light as best as possible, leaving the rest less important.
You could gain the whole world but loose your soul in the process
and end up with what—death.
Make God your foundation and rock, and let the rest follow after.
—J. Micheal Dekle

Mindset

Keeping a positive mindset will give you a 50% chance of
succeeding automatically.
Meaning if you prepare,
Stay focus,
Keep moving forward no matter what,
You will have another 49% chance of succeeding.
Leaving 1% to not.
That's a pretty good odd of succeeding.
—J. Micheal Dekle

Old Home

Memories made,
And days played.
Special moments seen and discovered.
Passing away days of such a place we called good old sweet home.
We are thankful for how she blew.
With nobody having to calling cold gone blue.
Just passing away memories and photos of the good old golden day's views.
Now recreating it all in love and hope.
New locations,
New ideas,
New visions,
New reminders.
New in all, but us.
Leaving us to travel on in different places,
But as one family forever.
For love sings on,
forever
&
Forever
Amen.
—J. Micheal Dekle

To Love

To love someone is to have an admiration,
A curious desire to hear just a little bit more from them.
To feel as though you are racing each other to out do each other,
So you challenge,
Thus motivate one another,
Always backing up one another though.
To always stay self aware of yourself,
To look and act your best.
To be nervous over little things,
For pleasing one of other is constantly thought of.
Knowing no matter what happens, love will hold you together.
To accept and care.
To embrace any realities.
To know when to fight over something,
And when it's not important enough to.
To bring out the best in each other,
To let each other grow independently,
But supporting all the way.
To join life's,
To take a single road and turn it into a double one that soon
becomes one again, for you become with one,
But wider and bigger and stronger connected together.
That if sometimes the roads may detour off,
They always will come back.
To love is to admire, respect and always be there no matter what.
God is love, so all true love comes from God.
—J. Micheal Dekle

True Success

I have spoken with people who have been highly successful.
Such workaholics,
That they forget what fun is without working.
How to take a break to enjoy a precious moment.
They justify their actions by accomplishments,
Forgetting to accomplish the most important thing imaginable.
The meaning to life if all would fall and never be again.
They forget to balance their life and add value in love ones,
Some one day will awake having everything imaginably possible to share it with no one who truly loves them for them,
Who supported and cared for them to help build such a life,
That they will hate life,
Drinking it away,
Fading it away just for a pay check.
Leaving to beg, we all must have a balanced life to have a happy fulfilling one.
Family over money any day.
I would rather be mentally, spiritually and physically healthy than to own everything in the world.
The most precious things are invisible and are free.
Money is money; it has no true power really.
Money is like dirt and clay.
You need dirt and clay to make bricks to build something, but you need wisdom to first know how to make the bricks.
—J. Micheal Dekle

Colors

I have learned that people will show different colors all the time.
Some days they will show worst colors than others.
But you don't claim someone is a certain way,
By one bad color they have shown.
You have to pay attention which ones they always fall back to,
And try to be and show the most.
Everyone is growing,
Meaning as long as they deep down are trying to show their best colors,
you know they are only trying to be genuine and real and overall have a good heart.
—J. Micheal Dekle

Words Impact

Choose carefully the words you use.
For they are your imagination,
Are all what someone will walk away with.
So they also are your imagine.
Be gentle,
Kind and loving.
Swearing only discredits yourself,
For it's unnecessarily used.
Use words that have pure power.
Have true inspiration.
For then people will take you more seriously.
For you only showed love,
So they have to,
Or they will walk away ashamed they were the smaller person.
—J. Micheal Dekle

Teamwork

When you can find someone who will help you achieve your goals,
You will see just how cripple you were by yourself.
One can be brilliant,
But another can see and say different opinions to help give feed back.
Team work solves problems,
Lessens stress & helps improve one another.
You just have to see yourself as family,
Trust worthy and honest.
Truthful and polite.
Respectable to be respected.
And willing to listen to learn.
—J. Micheal Dekle

Find Yourself

Once you find yourself,
Life can truly begin.
For you understand who you are.
So the foundational grounds of who you stand as is made.
Don't become to selfish,
But rather know you have your own pathway that nobody can be,
But you.
Allow yourself to live, and enjoy life, and allow others to be apart of it.
Find love,
For love can drive your passion even further,
The power of love can transform and make you someone you didn't know you even could become.
Love yourself,
But not too much,
Or you will become blinded to your areas of need of adjusting, etc.
It's why finding someone who's truly true and honest is a must!
—J. Micheal Dekle

Vibes

Life will always give you 'bad vibes'
You can't be scared of it.
You must watch it carefully and ask yourself why do I think I feel a bad vibe?
Is it me second guessing myself?
Is it me suggesting some negativity to keep me away from my happiness?
Is it I'm just scared of some parts of myself,
Because I just don't fully understand it yet,
So I turn off those emotions.
Running away,
Thinking it's justifying it,
By dodging it,
When I'm only making my world smaller by not just taking that faith and leaning onto the positive fully,
Making it beautiful no matter what.
I fight for that positive.
For life's a fight to stay positive.
—J. Micheal Dekle

Your Belief

Some will believe something they tell themselves that nothing anybody does will change their mind,
For they believe it so much.
Even if that means it'll leave them missing out on an opportunity.
Their stubbornness ruins them.
Their disbelief in we all deserve happiness,
Holds them prisoner.
That people can be forgiven.
That some people never give up on love.
That if they would just stop being afraid,
They will fly and become stronger and braver than ever before.
But by each lie told to themselves that they believe.
They are only hurting and trapping their own self's from life's precious opportunities.
—J. Micheal Dekle

Lemonade

Forget yesterday if it only gave you lemons –
It has already forgotten you.
Don't sweat tomorrow –
You haven't even met yet.
Instead,
Open your eyes and your heart to a truly precious gift—
Today —
And only remember and hold on to your love ones,
And the things that lift you up.
If it brings you down,
Understand why,
Either fix it,
Adjust it,
Or don't worry about it until you know how to fix it.
Time fixes all things if allowed.
Our generation has forgotten about the gift of fixing.
It's rarely ever possible something isn't fixable.
We just are lazy and rather find or buy something different.
The highest level intelligence is admitting when you're wrong,
And allowing yourself to be corrected and become better.
—J. Micheal Dekle

Ghostly

Sometimes you have to wonder if you're a ghost,
And you're only playing a game with your imagination.
For you read a lot,
But see no direct action.
So you live more inside your mind than anywhere else.
—J. Micheal Dekle

Impulse

Many times,
People act on impulse.
Which isn't always a bad thing.
But sometimes it can make them say or do things that later down the road they regret.
Always think of others before self,
Because it works as a safety net,
Reason is: the second you think of others first, you naturally put yourself into theirs shoes and you're more likely going to treat them kinder and nicer.
Pride or self is always going to be your biggest downfall, for
After a while you will become narrow minded.
—J. Micheal Dekle

Fear

It's crazy what fear can do.
What disbelieve can do.
It's more crazy how we lie to ourselves,
By doubting what we deserve.
We all deserve nothing.
But are so freely given so much.
That it's mind blowing to hear someone say they do not deserve a gift someone is freely giving.
It's like telling God you don't deserve another breath,
And you would be correct.
But He loves you so much,
He gives you it.
It's the same way about love.
You can't tell someone who they can give their heart to,
They just give it.
There isn't such a thing as a perfect person, besides Jesus.
Meaning you only have to be willing to accept what they offer.
And grow together.
If you don't want to grow,
Or want to grow by your own,
You are only falling into another hole,
That at first will seem okay,
But the further you go,
The harder it will be to come back to love others,
For you will be consumed by your own self,
That nobody will ever be good enough for you.
For you have to many walls up.
Accept love people give you.
Accept Jesus's love for you, for He died innocently so you may be saved, that is love.
—J. Micheal Dekle

Value of Love

If you love something you never let it go,
Unless it's an item.
If it's a person,
You never can let it go.
For if you do,
Then you never even loved them to begin with.
Some think letting a person go is out of love.
As in some feel they do not deserve such a love from someone,
When in reality,
You can't limit the amount of love you can give to a person.
As you grow,
The love grows.
Never let go of love,
Rather pass it on if it's an item.
If it's someone,
Fight for the love,
Fight, fight until your dead.
That's love.
Never giving up on someone.
Sometimes we must walk away.
But true love can't leave the heart.
The love just transfers on to someone else.
That's Jesus's love.
He loves you so deeply He will never let you go,
He will only wait for you to come to Him.
—J. Micheal Dekle

The Heart

The heart is a treasure box.
Each heart has its differences.
Each heart holds its different treasures.
But once something enters into the heart.
It's forever imprinted,
Thus locked,
Stored,
Forever.
Yes, the heart can change over time.
But it takes much stress,
Much pain too,
And much love.
The heart can grow cold,
Or grow warm.
Treasure your heart,
Be careful.
Show love,
So your heart will explode with warmth.
With kindness.
With love that lasts forever.
—J. Micheal Dekle

Rock bottom

Some days we will struggle to want to take our next breath.
Some days we will reach such a rock bottom feeling,
That nothing matters but survival.
It's why we can't ever lose ourselves in these phases of moments.
If we do,
We can fall backwards so far.
Can discredit are own reflection.
Can hurt people without trying too,
In these moments all you think about is self.
For self has this living drive to move forward always.
Has this forever drive to want to live.
We must rid ourselves from such negatives that enter into our minds.
And remember love,
Compassion,
And what our true mission is.
Which is to share love.
Gods forever lasting love.
Share it in our beings,
Through our actions.
Love.
For life will always be more fulfilling.
—J. Micheal Dekle

Yearly Reflection

Look at yourself just from a year ago.
Now imagine yourself in a year.
It's funny how life does that to you.
Rings bells, memories and moments.
But usually we can be so into the moment that once the moments gone and you step away and reflect it all,
You're blown away.
Life happens so fast.
It's remarkably amazing how we forget that though.
How precious our time truly is.
It's why doing what you can to better yourself for tomorrow is a must.
To live life to its fullest possible that you are able to is a must.
I'm not meaning in a foolish fun way,
But in a successful way of being simply you.
The fun all comes as the journey moves forth.
Live for today.
Live as though it is your last day.
Live like you will forever and you will.
You will do and act on things with passion, which such motives that it stands out forever.
You will love to live life to help others,
To live by Gods ways.
For then when you have those reflection moments.
The understanding behind it all will just make that much more sense.
It's funny how life is,
How God is.
A year from today,
I just can't wait to be blown away by the amazing things that will have taken place.
It's visions like that,
That give life meaning.
Take one step at a time.
No matter how small it is.
Never give up.
Only try harder.

—J. Micheal Dekle

Viewpoints

I reach into my pocket to grab the sunglasses I want to wear.
I do so randomly.
Put them on,
Feeling, seeing hate,
Murder and crime.
Switch them out:
Look out feeling nothing,
Just this feeling of emptiness.
Switch them out once again:
Seeing love,
Feeling it,
But with it comes in the pity.
Some days these sunglasses choose which one will be seen,
And the person who chooses this is you.
So how you viewing life?
—J. Micheal Dekle

Guaranteed

While not much in life is truly guaranteed,
A lot actually is.
The beauty behind each precious soul is this.
You choose how you mentally feel,
And how your going to enact that out into your actions.
I have been so blessed to watch countless people act and seen their behavior through out it all.
Little did they know I was paying the upmost attention taking mental notes.
Reflecting it back at my own imagine and seeing how I have enacted by emotional feelings.
Yes, in a physical way life can be hard,
Can be even almost pure deadly.
But on an emotional level,
It's all choices.
It's all what you will allow to let in.
Stay positive;
Stay lifting others up higher.
For by doing so,
You're riding a wave in life that will take you across oceans, across deserts.
When those incredibly horrible bad times do come, you have such a high wave,
That when you surf down a little,
You have enough speed to shoot straight back up!
Count your blessings.
Know you are loved!
So beloved by God!
—J. Micheal Dekle

Push

Sometimes saying or doing those things that terrify us is what brings us alive.
Is what pushes us to understand life a little bit more.
It allows us to grow.
There are many ways in doing something.
There are many ways to express things also.
Sometimes doing the smallest things are the biggest things.
When you tell someone something,
Sometimes words can express it better at first than actions.
Sometimes the words are the actions.
Even sadly sometimes no words are an action.
When it comes to love,
If someone loves you,
They will understand you,
And take you where you are.
You just have to let them know.
So they know where you stand.
For together we can stand incredibly strong.
Alone we can also, but we won't be as strong.
Love is my song,
I sing it in my heart,
So when those days come where I feel I may fall apart,
I don't,
But start again to conquer life and love.
—J. Micheal Dekle

Love Rules

There are no rules in the game of love.
The only true rule is love.
It's that simple.
Love with all your heart.
Love with such a passion that everything good happens from within you.
For the love drives you to be so.
|Loyalty| Honestly | Forgiveness|
|Long Suffering | Selflessness | Kindness|
| Patients |
Ultimately
|Love|
Love transforms all.
—J. Micheal Dekle

Genuine Love

You can never be used if all you want to do is love.
You can never overly love,
For love has no limitations.
Even if you know you're being used,
You can only have pity on someone who would lower themselves to that.
You can only show kindness and love.
For it will set them free if they allow it.
So the example of being such,
Will never be a waste.
Yes, it may take some time for someone to learn that,
Maybe even a life time,
But one day they will.
And then the love you planned then will ring out and sing in their very beings,
They finally will understand what love is.
It's the highest most expensive quality to ever be given and to have.
But it's so beautiful,
For it's truly free if you let love sing and ring out.
Love.
—J. Micheal Dekle

Forever Love

Love never dies.
If you love someone,
You always will.
Sometimes we must love from afar.
Not because we want too.
But love doesn't force.
Doesn't even push.
It only knocks.
I will always love some from afar.
Praying everyday for them,
As I do for everyone.
Loves my motto.
Loves the key.
In love we trust!
In God we trust!
God | Love
Life
—J. Micheal Dekle

Over Obsessively Done

Sometimes we can get to overly obsessive with things or people.
That's not always a bad thing.
But if you get so obsessed with something that it starts bringing you down,
You must catch yourself.
Stop yourself,
And know all good things come in good time.
That you worrying or fighting for something won't bring it any sooner.
It'll be like ordering a package from somewhere and telling them you want it in five minutes when it's over 3,000 miles away.
It's just not possible.
So why let it bother you,
Why worry, you shouldn't.
Just let it go to a place in your mind that it won't bother you.
Have patience.
When it comes to life and love,
I personally am lucky,
I have a lot of passions which equals love.
Sometimes I get too catch up on certain things; things that only time has to take it place,
But I have decided there's nothing I can do, but wait.
So why let it bother me?
I won't let it ruin me from accomplishing other passions in my life.
Yes, the wait is worth it for I love what I am doing.
Time won't ever change that easily, if it's a passion of yours.
If I would purely focus on one passion in life, I would go crazy, for all good things take time to develop.
Same applies when it comes to relationships.
You have to balance it all out.
If you spend to much time with one person over another you will have an unbalanced relationship, friendship etc.
Learn which battles to fight and which to let go.
For if there's absolutely nothing you can do about it,
Then why let it control you?
Just wait until it happens,

Or until the other reaches out if it's in a relationship.
If they don't,
Love them still,
But it tells you they never cared or loved you like you did them.
Yes, it's possible to love those who don't love you.
Remember that.
—J. Micheal Dekle

Church

Going to church won't save you.
Going to church won't even protect you.
Only Jesus can save you and protect you.
A church is a hospital.
Everyone there is damaged and hurt.
Going to church is a place to associate with other people like you.
People who have a deep desire to learn more about God and His love. To talk and understand God in a deeper better way.
Yes, we all live and have different struggles we face.
But a church isn't a place to socialize like you do in public mall.
It's a place to grow, support, love, and come closer together.
Many churches now days forget all of this.
Sadly, many church you walk in and just want to walk right back out.
For it's as walking into a high school.
There are clicks and small groups.
People are antisocial; anti-you.
Find a church where love and truth is talked about and never leave.
—J. Micheal Dekle

The Fallen Risen

Some days my emotions ride me like a bronco.
In these moments I have to remember what really matters.
What will past, and what will stay.
Leaving me to regret much,
But at the end of the day,
As I lay—
I float off into a dream land,
A place we call heaven.
Where all peace and love dwells.
It lifts my soul and spirt high; very so,
Leaving me to reopen my eyes sadden.
Sadden that I can't reflect such a perfect image as the one I feel.
For If I could,
I believe it would light this world up so brightly,
That we would understand just how bright God is.
How bright angels really are.
Why Gods light would kill us.
Why angels terrify us.
And just how fallen we have become.
If we could walk and show the light we carry,
I believe many would burn brighter than the sun.
And others darker than the darkest abysses.
For it's our hearts that shine light.
Our words and actions guide what our hearts feel.
Leaving some days our hearts are filled with much love,
And other days much selfishness.
And some days both,
Leaving an imperfect light to show.
Which is most of us.
Leaving us as the fallen,
But also the called.
The beloved.
That if we try our hardest to shine love,
It may not be perfect, but God will make it perfect for those who need it most.

Sharing

Some days I like to share a lot,
Other days,
I feel like sharing little.
I tie it into how we sometimes let our feelings over power us,
Limiting us from being someone unforgettable.
If we bottle ourselves up to wallow in ourselves,
How can anyone else ever share themselves with us,
If they don't even know us,
How are they going to interact among us?
Leaving us a smaller bubble.
Be a huge bubble.
A bubble of love.
—J. Micheal Dekle

Beauty in Life

Life's beautiful!
I take all I see and enlighten it with energy of love.
Only then can I see this world in still pure living beauty.
There's still beauty in this beast.
Around every corner,
You just have to have the eyes to see it.
The spirit to receive it.
And the love to spread it!
—J. Micheal Dekle

New Beginnings

Let's start a conversation that never has an ending.
Let's start a new beginning.
Let's be us and forget everything else.
Let's pave a pathway that leads us home to each other's arms
everyday, knowing our true home is in Heaven.
Every time.
Let's do life living freely as us.
Welcome me,
Welcome the new beginning of my world with Jesus Christ and
God guiding.
Branching out with love and kindness.
For negativity has been my view for to long.
No more shall I let it define and guide me.
Rather let it warn me time to time.
For negativity does has it place for sin still lives on.
I choose to never be naive, rather balanced.
—J. Micheal Dekle

You Choose Life's View

Life will always be how you make it.
I mean I don't care if you're in the middle of a tornado—
If your mind is saying,
"Oh yes, oh man yes this is thrilling!"
Well it will be!
If your like,
"Oh God, I'm going to die!"
Well your last seconds will be of fear instead of thrilling loving
heart-racing excitement!
Life's 90% mind set,
And 10% everything else.
—J. Micheal Dekle

Love is In Us

Let love be us.
Let everyone love.
Let me be me.
Let you be you.
Let us sing of life and love.
I'm for you and you sure know God is too!
Lets adore and admire,
To be inspired and empowered to climb every tower of love.
Let me climb Love,
And explain every bit as I climb.
Let's join in hand and run hand in hand and be us forever more.
Come in,
Let us join in some fun.
Lets run with life and see it as a race car and take us afar to the stars.
Let us go to places, places don't know,
Let us join in on love.
Let us run away from evil and never come back again.
Lets be friends,
Best friends forever.
God is love,
So the love I run after is from above.
—J. Micheal Dekle

God is Love

I look up thanking God for another day of life.
For giving me a deeper sense to life.
For forgiving me with grace and mercy from all my wrong doings.
For protecting me in those dark times.
For giving me insightful light to light my pathway so I do not fall.
For providing me with my daily bread so I do not go hungry.
For helping me to become a braver me—a more loving kind genuine soul who isn't selfish no more, rather trying to be selfless because Gods example has taught me.
For never leaving me when He should of just left me to die.
For helping me to understand His love just that much more so I can share His love with those I run across.
For sending Jesus to die for us, so we can become the righteous.
Giving us His Words in His Bible to help guide us home to Heaven.
For sending life problems that teach patiences, discipline, long suffering and forgivingness.
God is love,
His love is for us.
So we are loved beyond words to express.
—J. Micheal Dekle

Thank you for choosing to read another of my books. I hope and pray you were blessed by these words. Life's an adventure, and we are always growing and becoming someone better. We all have been and still go through life's struggles. It is nice to know we are not the only ones, that many of us face such troubles all the time. For more positive empowering words: Follow one of my blogs Via **Instagram** —
@jonnyslifeview

@sirknightwrites

@j.loveforeveru

@swiftnewsblog

Thank You For Reading
May love always carry us on through any storm that comes our way.
#LoveOn

www.ingramcontent.com/pod-product-compliance
Lightning Source LLC
Chambersburg PA
CBHW081353040426
42450CB00016B/3420